Barefoot Poetess

Paris Rosemont

WestWords Books

www.westwords.com.au
41 Hunter Street, Parramatta NSW 2150 Australia.

Published by WestWords Limited 2025.

A catalogue record for this
book is available from the
National Library of Australia

ISBN: 978-1-923044-45-6
Cover design by Sailor Studio

Printed and bound by Ligare book printers
Distributed in Australia by Peribo

My love —
this is all I have
to give

it is not much
but it is *everything*

A note from the *Barefoot Poetess*

The term *poetess* seems to have vanished from contemporary vernacular – presumably for very good reason. Indeed, I am grateful for the fortitude of women who paved the way for me.

But I like the term. To me, *poetess* feels wild and whimsical, seductive, and a little dangerous. I like the illicit feeling of it in my mouth, the way it teases the back of my teeth.

I have reclaimed *poetess* as an act of rebellion.

Introduction

Where to start with this big, beautiful heartbreak of a collection? This is confessional poetry in all its glorious exhibitionism — a real *fuck you* to all those trying to lock the poem in a gilded cage. Who else in Australia would dare such flushes, both erudite and street-wise in equal measure? In *Barefoot Poetess* Rosemont makes accessible haibuns, haikus, sonnets, odes, prose poems, laments, fourteeners and even invented forms like the raucous 69er.

With a loving attention to the red-hot raw heat of revving Kawasakis, thumb wars that define school yards, hair and make-up backlots and dysfunctional relationships with just enough kink to maintain a spark, Rosemont offers serious attention to all those details we might otherwise discard as unserious, not quite poetic enough — often too damn salacious. Meanwhile, she imagines us into worlds where a robot replaces a mother, *The Colombo Plan* is an underground cartel and Jesus is a super star — and gosh, it's hard to date him.

As such, Rosemont reinvigorates the claim that poetry is a means by which to not only notice and to attend to, but also to play, play, play. This is a collection unafraid of itself from a poet unwilling to bend to any whim but her own.

As Rosemont writes, 'love is a many splintered thing'.
And indeed, I am splintered; I am still pulling the barbs out.

Tim Loveday

Barefoot Poetess

Mama's flown away with the mockingbirds

'The mortgage of the dead is known...'
~ Carson McCullers (The Mortgaged Heart)

The children know I died weeks ago. This corpse
masquerading as their mother is an imposter.
Noone else has cottoned on yet. But I raised
savvy kids. They *know*.

The Other smooths their chestnut cowlicks as she
readies them for school, but she does not press
their ham and cheese sandwiches with the novelty
brontosaurus cutter, serving no purpose other
than to spread smiles. There's no more steam
in this vintage cast iron for the luxury of delight.

I pity these wretched orphans. Imagine
how unsettling it must feel to be sung
to sleep by a ghost who knows
their favourite lullabies and looks so
like someone they once knew.

Hush little babies, don't you cry

don't tell anyone that your mama has died.

They reach out to touch her — so convincing is she that she could *almost* be real. But their desperate hands swipe through air. *It's a virtual reality game!* They're grappling with a hologram. Whirling with the ethereal weightlessness of a floating dancer, their mother has brokered a fool's-gold escape. She has mortgaged her heart. The cost of her wings — two tiny souls.

Diagnosis: ekphrasis

~A haibun after Sarah Jane's 'Silhouette'

watercolours bleed
feathered sure-lined silhouettes
rorschachesque inkblots

How to carve a poet out of a pumpkin: with great care. Or none at all. Be sure to wear latex gloves, a fishmonger's apron, goggles, galoshes. They bleed a lot. Find a nerve. Make an incision. Oh, watch how they gush and splatter onto the butcher's paper. Now read the splotches like carmine-tinted tea leaves. Of course they carry deeper meanings. It is up to you to find out what.

it's a butterfly
(did you just yawn?) sorry i
don't excite you more

Thank fuck this illegitimate haibun is starting to take shape. Sometimes I worry about my well running dry, you know? Like when will I write my *last good poem?* Has it already been written? As a poet of just two years, six months and 28 days (give or take) it seems a little sad to potentially already be a washed-out *has-been*. Then again, better than being a *never-was*. So anyhow, this well — it's still wet.

obviously a fan-
tailed shell *(an oyster?)* dribbling
pearlescent mucous

Upon closer inspection of her anatomy, the flesh is more pert than languidly-spread oyster flaps. More like a tight mussel — whiskered pubes and all. Did you know that some bivalve molluscs mass-reproduce in a phenomenon called 'broadcast spawning'? It's one gigantic sea orgy: a salty, foaming free-for-all potluck. Perhaps I need to step away from the doomscrolling, 'cos now I can't unsee the footage of this synchronised trickle of white *–not unlike the human kind–* drifting out on the tide, possibly at the very beach I swim in. It wouldn't be the first time I gag on something foreign I've swallowed. I hadn't even been actively searching. The algorithm '*Suggested [it] for [Me]*'. What do you think that says about me, doc?

the c-word. i can't
bring myself to say it. no,
not 'cunt' — *worse* — 'cancer'

So, the scare really scared me. I'd been almost ready to go by my own hand. Then **chuckle* *snort* *oh, what a plot twist** fate thought it'd be a lark to take that choice away from me. I realised I wasn't ready to go after all. Not like that. Quick and clean would have been my modus operandi. Nobody wants an ugly death.

i see a vulva
inside a breast. i'm aroused.
does this mean i'm queer?

I'm talking about my sexuality, Herr Doktor[1], not my peculiarity. Though there is no doubting that I am indeed a strange little bird. *Do I terrify?*

The final stanza is a nod to both Sylvia Plath's *Lady Lazarus* and Anaïs Nin's *Little Birds.*

Location scouting

'… this temptation to step off the edge and fall weightless, away from the world'
~ Dorianne Laux (For the Sake of Strangers)

I could name the precise location — the exact clifftop I've got picked out. Past the jagged tip where the waves pound like restless spirits of drowned asylum-seekers roaring across the *Pacific* in tins of *King Oscar* sardines, banging against this impenetrable wall: *let us in!*

The crags of stripy rock are quite beautiful up close. They remind me of cream layered wedges of choc-hazelnut torte from that trendy continental bakery on the main drag of Campbell Parade, the name of which I can no longer recall because we always used to refer to it simply as *the cherry strudel shop*.

I am exposed to the elements out on this grassy knoll. I like the feeling of the wind whipping my unbound hair into wild obsidian serpents. I stop—though my vipers continue their untamed mazurka, lashing my cheeks like a cat o' nine tails. The edge has abruptly vanished into a sheer drop. As a twice-removed cousin of more popular beaches up the coast–*Bondi, Bronte, Maroubra*–here there is no fencing for the safety of tourists. No lookouts or guardrails. With a belt-loop of some 34,000 kilometres hugging Australia's hefty girth, one cannot expect the *entire* coastline to be rabbit-proofed.

Today is not the day. Though if it were, it would *still* not be the day (it would happen at night). I continue ambling down the hill, around the bend, past boxy houses. A stormwater drain has burst. My nose inadvertently crinkles at the stench of raw sewage. I hold my breath until I am down a narrow flight of speckled stone steps, where the landing opens up into the goblet arc of Gordon's Bay. I spent knobbly-kneed summers here, barefoot, rock-hopping in the shallows, dive-bombing in the deep, afterwards shaking sand out of my *everywhere*, and wearing the tan lines of my summer like a tattooed swimsuit right through to mid-winter.

My dearest, darling everything

I love your dextrous, strong and tender hands;
cartographer—keen circler of my maps.
How you adore me fierce, without demands
for me to bend or change till I relapse
to factory settings, bland as CO(g).
A thirsting fish, I thrash inside my bowl
all goggle-eyed and gasping at my need
for you. I'd give up civil rigmarole
to lick the knife's edge of your intellect.
No pleasure comes without a smidge of pain —
for you I'd gladly die the little death:
again, again, again, again, again!
And when I reach Saint Peter's Gates above,
I shall festoon hot entrails of my love.

Jesus Christ, it's not easy dating a superstar

I don't take a seat at your supper table alongside your
100 fresh disciples fawning over your *lilac wine* party trick again.
I'm not captured in Da Vinci's mural, though I lurk in the
sidelines feigning cucumber indifference. You don't want

the Magdalenes to get jealous. I watch Medusa-eyed as you
send little love hearts to your Insta(nt) fans as they flutter
their pretty emojis at you. How many of them slide
their slippery little cursors into your DMs, I wonder.
How many unsolicited tit pics

have you been sent? *How many have you wanked to?*
I could have booty-called a still-hot ex-lover or two, though
I broke up with them all in favour of you — a thousand miles
away, penetrating a thousand times deeper
into the hea(r)t of me. You — with your adoring harem.

You — who will only love me in shadows. How they fondle
you in their fingers, admiring
you like a gem, twisting you this way and that, to bathe
in your refracted radiance. They tuck
you under their wicked little tongues like the body of Christ,
uttering lustful Hail Marys.

Meanwhile, I am jack(ing off)-
in-the-box pressed
into a coffin, straining
against tightly coiled
serpentine springs.
When the lid
comes
off, I ejaculate
cobra-like
a sunflower
shooting
for a star

Proshchaniye, Ms Karenina

You turned me into a petrol sniffer. Pressed oxytocin-laced
denim to my face til I fell
                                        trembling into your waiting arms.

Rosebud. Rosehip. Rohypnol. *Hyp…hyp…*
you hypnotise me…
hit me up.   *I'm begging you.*   Go on, hit me.

Squeezing every last drop from this oily rag,
my kerchief has fallen onto the tracks and a train is careening
        towards me   *[Screeeeeeccccccchhhhhh!]*

I move towards the very thing

                                        that will obliterate me.

The Colombo Plan

My father arrived in Australia on *The Colombo Plan*.
Inventing a backstory for myself more exciting than
my dime-a-dozen migrant yarn, I started the rumour
that *TCP* was an underground cartel, adding with Oscar-
worthy flourish that if people messed with our *family*,
they might be *next*. They already saw me as a dog-eating chink;
regarded me with suspicion and … *was that the tom yum tang*
of fear? It worked for a while, till Jade called my bluff.
Her father was an *actual* policeman. At risk of him launching
a drug bust, I had to kill the rumour, declaring breezily one day
that my father had retired from the game and was now working
a muggle job
as a taxi driver.

Fresh out of university in the early 1970s, the recipient
of a foreign exchange
scholarship, my father had packed a small hard-shelled
Samsonyte of his humble
belongings, boarded a plane with a one-way ticket and landed
not in his vision
of snow-capped mountains or verdant green hills alive
with *Edelweiss*, but in a sunburnt

country where locals *slip, slop, slapped* his back, declaring
She'll be right, even though he was out
of his depth in a foreign country
armed with little in his pocket
and even less *Engrish.*

My father had a degree in *Physics* back home. A professor and
author of a popular crib-note chapbook on *electro-*
magnetism — though these bits of foreign
paper were worthless in this *lucky* country.
Taxi-driving had its utility. What you don't learn from textbooks
is the local lingo. From his late-night callouts, he picked up
pissed passengers retiring
from *piss-ups*. Some were *piss-weak* as they slumped
close to passing out on the sticky vinyl seats
of the split-toned Holden Kingswood he was renting-to-buy.
Others were *pissed off* in their state
of inebriation. He drew the line at *pissing*. He had a strict
No Pissing in Taxi policy.

As a daughter of *piss-poor* migrants, I was force-fed stories
of sacrifice like a goose being primed for its *foie gras* fate. Everything

my parents had suffered and given up and left behind for me
was shoved down my throat. *She'll be right.* I guess
they were preparing me for the realities of life.
Girls need to learn how to shut up and swallow.
I was relieved when my brother was born four years later.
I now had someone to play pass-the-parcel with.
Share a bit of the:

> ~~(a) Love*~~
> (b) Guilt
> (c) Shame
> (d) Self-loathing
> (e) All of the above.

* I would happily have shared the Love
had there been enough of it to go around, but it was scarce
as hen's teeth and I had recurring nightmares
of all my Henny-Penny teeth falling out.
Night after night, I'd wake drenched
in sweat to the image of my own Edvard Munch
reflection scream-grinning toothlessly at me.
It was just a dream. She'll be right.

But for all the deals my parents had to make
with pasty foreign devils in crisp white-
collared suits to buy me
a life they never had, still —
(ungrateful bitch that I am)
I was not alright.
Not then.
Not now.
Not even close.

doppelgänger dildo

(i) tea with tony

the first time i met tony was at my home. i'd invited him to tea. he'd accepted.
won't bore you with backstory. except to say i'd grown up poring over newsprint
photographs tony had taken of rock gods in *drum media*. suddenly, everything in
my house seemed too shabby — *myself included*. not everything is a quick fix,
so i did what i could: went and bought a royal albert tea set from *peter's
of kensington*. each fine floral china cup was a dainty pastel gold-
gilded dream. vessels of what i longed to be instead of this
gaudy, chipped-lipped, rainbow-striped mug from a box
of six *on sale!* in the discount bin out the front
of *victoria's basement*. tony compliments
the tea set. *oh, this old thing?!* i say,
waving a breezy hand. i grin to myself. that's $529 well spent!

(ii) poetry with pip

a decade later, i'm sitting in my first poetry class since high school. this week's homework is to write a two-sentence poem about *a daily private indiscretion*. so it is that my vibrator poem comes into being. obliquely titled *the hum of escape,* i present it to class like a manx proudly proffering freshly mauled vermin. pip is aghast. never in all her years of teaching has she had a student write about *this* as part of the exercise. i wear this statement like a badge of pride. she feels the need to clarify that by setting the task, she had been expecting disclosures in the vein of *i scoff chocolate after the kids have gone to bed* kinda thing. paris rosemont: making poetry tutors blush since 2022.

(iii) shooting stars

i am performing *the hum of escape* to a live backing track: rhythmic pulsations
of my doppelgänger on a pleasing *mode 6, speed 4* (not my setting for private
purposes with my non-stunt-double). it goes down **badum** **tish** a treat.
i like the audience's gasps of *is that…? is she really…?* before they whip out
their phones so they can show it to their friends later.
ali uses astronomical terms
to describe what is happening to me. words like: *SKYROCKETING* and
METEORIC RISE in BIG EXCITED CAPS alongside rocketship emojis.
my head is spinning from whiplash. usually, one must be ~*yea*~ tall
to ride this ride. i managed to sneak under the barrier when no-one was looking.
so here i am at knox street bar; a bastard
amongst purebreds. the bouncers eye me up and down.
i am skittish with nerves. but i am wearing my fuck-off, fuck-me
thigh-high stiletto boots. muscles part for me. i play hooky after intermission,
escaping into the dark enclave of a makeshift green room.
my lover goes down on me whilst the barman
pretends to be polishing glasses.

(iv) back to tony

as a teenager, i had a poster of björk up on my wall.

that iconic one, where she is winking at the camera, face

scrunched, looking like a weird little top-knotted pixie

immortalised through tony's lens. over copious cups of lady grey tea

and my homemade lemon curd tartlets

i am regaled with tales that haven't *all* stayed on the road.

like the time tony instructs björk to simply be her usual

quirky self at the shoot. peering up at him with childlike naïveté, head

cocked and eyes squinting against sunlight, in her lilting icelandic

cadence, she coos *you tink i'm quirrrky?* grins mischievously and winks.

click *that's the beauty of it you see,* tony explains to me. *the really quirky*

people don't even realise they are. they just are.

Kill the Wabbits

Three little kits appeared one morning in the back corner of Hop's hutch,
writhing sightless as moles in the straw, pink as the little piggies
on my baby brother's smooth, un-walked-on feet, hairless as a Brazilian
sauntering barefoot along the breezy Copacabana.

I didn't realise till well into adulthood that those plump
little piggies weren't on their way to *shop* at the markets, armed
with plaid-lined picnic baskets swinging in the crooks of their chubby
Michelin arms. The ol' cad Hip had gone in for the snip a week prior;
evidently not before shooting a bullseye. These mewling miracles
were a surprise to us all.

Hop was unprepared for motherhood; rejected the wriggling worms
as though she'd had an unwanted teen pregnancy like those you
hear about on the telly, where the ditzy girl hadn't even known
she'd been pregnant — thought she'd simply been bloated and crampy
the night a baby plops into the toilet bowl
out the back of Chick-fil-A.

I'd tried to save the orphaned souls. They didn't make it through the night.
I found their bodies huddled together, frozen stiff under the heat lamp.
Gave them a shoebox burial in our backyard under the blood
orange tree that was still just a sapling. Cried for a week
over their lost souls and my survivor's guilt. My then-husband
told me I was being silly. That it was simply the nature
of nature and I was foolish for wasting my salt
on such expendable creatures. I guess that should have prepared me
for when I lost our child in the womb a couple of years later.
Chastising my tears on Mother's Day, he said *but you weren't even*
a mother yet.

Creatures of the deep

I'd always been a solo gourami.
You materialised—like a macroscopic
Ecuadorian kelp forest transforming
my barren reef.

You weren't anything like the siren
I'd conjured in my sea-faring fantasies
of sandy-beach cocktails plumed
with paper umbrellas, sipping gaily
as the sun dipped beneath a coco cabaña.

Instead, you were jelly-limbed, silvery
strands framing your coralline
beam. It was that smile of yours
that first disarmed me. Like a star-
gazer, I'd watch as plankton in your orbit
were swept along your gravitational
current, smiles multiplying around
you like bioluminescent blooms.

The ocean swells — you fill
the squid-inked horizon. Gentle
giant of the sea, oblivious
to your own magnificence. You glide
through rolling tides with your calming
frequencies: creaks, codas, clicks,
echolocating…*echo*…*echo*…

All creatures become weightless
in water. Your whale song holds me
in suspense. And soon, I too am ankle-
deep, knee-deep, chest-deep, *in deep.*

We swim — fin to fin. I grow
amorphous, a companion
fish that can finally stop fearing
creatures of the deep. I fall
into stroke with you as we glide
together through the twisting
ribbons of light, pausing only
to breach the undulating
surface. I hold my breath—
you catch yours. And like a fat
gold hourglass pivoting, time
stands still. The world is over-
turned. We begin again.

Foot and spouse disease

I used to hate his feet. They were a size larger than standard-sized shoes in standard shoe shops. I had to source specialty shoes to house his too-muchness. Hardened heels, dry and cracked as the Nullarbor Plain, with yellowed nails so thick they required the purchase of extra-large nail clippers. He was a large man; unable to bend down past his Clausian gut. Thus, the task of taking heavy-duty garden shears to his gnarled undergrowth fell upon me. The *snip snip snip* of nail clippers still sends me into flashbacks of his hooves-for-toes, clumped together tight as a spring-trap.

The air down there did not get proper ventilation. It became a swamp of sweat and sludge which, in the moshpit of stinking summers, housed in the steel-capped sauna of his work boots, would become a bacterial orgy. I'd slide my slender fingers, lubed with tinea cream, in between each of his toes. Had I been a foot fetishist, such slippery fingering may have aroused me. But as it was, it made me want to retch.

He was larger than life, this man. A figure looming colossal. Not as a Heracles might, but as a giant, casting shadows and fear. His tree-trunk legs would thunder down the hall and I would keep quiet as a mouse, hoping he would forget I was there. But he would sniff me out, grind my bones.

One day, a bun appeared in my oven. As it rose, so too did hope. The giant had clumsy, oafish feet with big toes so very big they were the size of our newborn's entire perfectly pink, perfectly formed toes all combined. My trivial concerns floated away like a helium balloon released into the sky. Somehow, out of the ash of our bones and keratin, and the Clag Paste of our liquefied salt, we had produced a thing of beauty. I'd shower with kisses the porcelain pads of our son's dainty feet. He'd wiggle his plump little toes, swollen as cornichons. As he lay on his back, squealing with delight, his body would curl inward like a contented armadillo. I finally discovered what love was.

Ode to virgin apple trees

YOU STAND in your shrouded rows, leafless limbs trembling as you are inspected — fondled to check whether you are ripe. You are not ready. Your budding breasts strain against your bridal veils, protecting your lithe, underdeveloped bodies. Little puckered nipples hint at ripening delights, standing to attention — brides of nature blossoming for your Master. He is waiting for you to come into season. He will harvest you. Your cheeks will flush as one by one, you are plucked. And you will tremble, you will tremble — at being stripped so bare. He likes the way you taste.

So he will take

and he will take

and he will take.

I found this jawbone at the sea's edge

~ after Ted Hughes's 'The Relic'

a perfect specimen encased
in stone; just a hint of saw-
tooth glinting pearl against charcoal
compressed sediments sandwiching
mineral and bone.

How came you to lie in your sea-
side tomb after centuries of voyaging through
amniotic womb cradling your languid hull?
Weightless through time until ship-
wrecked you rest your weary head
on pillows of sand, a rocky bed at the foot
of cliffs, howling wind-whipped as spiky
tufts of marram grass quiver. Ammonites
lay themselves in sacrificial offering fused
by your side in the hope of hitching
a ride with you into the next life.

Christmas Eve Shopping List

~ after Sylvia Plath's 'The Applicant'

First, are you my sort of person?
Do you have
Four eyes, a kind smile or a beard, prickly
Pear intellect to penetrate
Me like a pincushion,

Your key in my bowl? No, no? Then
How will I pick your lock?
Stop dallying.
Plunge into my bowl
Of punch-drunk love ready

To quench the desert
Of your dry July
And I'll show you a *ho*
Ho snow-white Christmas.
Will you love it?
It is guaranteed

To keep your motor running
And dissolve of sorrow.
We power chariots from the horsepower.
How about this Eve plucked

From a storm cloud —
A little bruised, but not a bad fit.
Will you love it?
It is waterproof, shatterproof, proof
That even the most tender of hearts
Will not stay broken.
Believe me, it will bloom again.

Now this book, excuse me, is empty.
I have the ticket for that.
Fill me with your ink — a pillow
Book. Well, what do you think
Of *that?* Naked as paper to start

But in twenty-five days I'll have a sleeve,
In fifty, a wetsuit dripping
Like a second skin. A living
Canvas, everywhere you look.

Lila's Mixtape of Lovers

(I) Arrested Development

~ Sitcom theme song

The ukelele strikes a chord — I
gush like a geyser — Pavlovian
response between my legs at the play-
ful strumming whilst my mind starts humming
in anticipation of what will
soon follow: your eager hands fumbling
beneath my skirt. You kiss my neck, lips,
other lips… We end up needing to
rewind half the episode we missed.

(II) 'They say you're a saint, you're a whore, you're a sinner, that he had you, he made you, he can't live without you he can't live without you'

~ Garbage

I should have slid overboard as soon
as my gut started sinking. Nothing
startling: you were unadventurous.
When a girl turns up to your hotel,
do you really need to ask what to
do next? You were all swagger, no balls.
They say size doesn't matter — that it's
how you use it. You were lacking in
both departments. I had to fake it.

(III) *'I'm flying so high off the ground when you're around'*

~Jem

I once found myself riding a cock-
pit simulator in an old war
aviation museum. Funny
how we acquire left of field interests
when we think we're in love. I sent you
pics; questioned your orientation
when you said: *those missiles are well hung!*

(IV) *'We're like creatures of the wind — and wild is the wind'*

~ Nina Simone

We were wild, you and I — ravenous
souls in search of deviant pleasures.
I would leash you at night and take you
for walks in the crisp autumn air, tug
you till you whimpered. I'd never heard
a grown man moan or beg as you did.
I eventually tired of you, cast
you adrift. On windy nights, I still
hear you howl my name amongst she-oaks.

(V) *'Lilac wine is sweet and heady, where's my love?'*

~ Jeff Buckley

I was charmed by your Eden, rustic
vines snaking around trellises like
exotic dancers swaying their juice-
y wares. Snap frozen, you said you'd pop
grapes inside me one day — extract them
with your tongue. After we broke up, I
wondered whether they were still preserved
in your Westinghouse, or if you were
sipping wine out of some other cunt.

(VI) *'In the land of Gods and Monsters I was an angel looking to get fucked hard'*

~ Lana Del Rey

I fell for you. Hard. In every way.
You took my innocence *(what was left
of it)*. You were both God and Monster —
convinced me to take a bite. I choked
on your cum-flavoured lies; thought I'd die.
Instead, I had my stomach pumped — purged
Mephistopheles. After you left,
I had to delete half my playlist.
You had ruined all my favourite songs.

This poem is contemporary twist on the poetic form 9 x 9 x 9
I call my constructed form a 69er: 6 stanzas x 9 lines, each line x 9 syllables.

sTilL CraZy AfteR aLL tHEse YeArs …
~ a (mostly) found poem

… is what the doctor said

psycho killer, qu'est-ce que c'est?

diminished responsibility:

a partial excuse to murder

excuse the static — the line is fuzzy

her blacks crackle and drag

form an orderly queue

behind the battered

women who kill. abnormal

minds, abnormal murderers

murderess is a strong word

to have attached to you

it rustles, like a taffeta skirt

murderess, murderess

Citations:
Title: D. Fraser, from S. Yeo 'Partial Excuses to Murder' (1990) p112
L1: J. Hunter & J. Bargen, ibid, p125
L2: Talking Heads 'Psycho Killer' lyrics
L3: Crimes Act 1900 (ACT), section 14: trial for murder—diminished responsibility
L4: S. Uniacke, from S. Yeo 'Partial Excuses to Murder' p1
L6: Sylvia Plath 'Edge'
L8-9: J. Tolmie, from S. Yeo 'Partial Excuses to Murder' p61
L9-10: J. Hunter & J. Bargen, ibid, p125
L11-14: Margaret Atwood 'Alias Grace'

Allswell that Endswell

'Do you bite
your thumb at us, sir? …
No, sir, I do not bite my thumb
at you, sir, but I bite my thumb, sir'
~ Shakespeare (Romeo and Juliet, Act I, Scene I)

I was today
years old when I learned
that *thumb* is rooted
in the Latin *tumere:* 'to swell'.
It all makes sense now — how
we raise perky thumbs
when things go well
as though miming
that's swell!

I have two thumbs
two Muses of Comedy
or Tragedy depending
on my whim like a score paddle
on *Dancing with the Stars*
or the Queen of Heart's
decree, I can signal
with a simple up
or down
whether
someone's head
will come
off. This kind
of power trip
could really make
one's head
swell

On idle days
my thumbs twiddle
other times they are at war
with head honchos
from rival hands
impassioned
war
cries echoing
like Braveheart
across schoolyards:
1…2…3…4…
I declare a thumb
WAR!

They're tools
little boys
wield to smugly
pull out
[plums]

Even blue
cowgirls do what
they gotta do. Uma Thurman
used what nature gave her
for high-
way pleasure
hitchhiking her way
across the galaxy

Technically
a non-finger
it's the Pluto of digits
holding entire
lifetimes within
each Milky Way
swirl

dusted
for prints: *evidence*
or inked: *proof*
of existence

Sometimes
a thumb
is just
a thumb
nothing more
nothing less

Oedipal
mistress
getting in between
a hammer and a nail
it all comes
back to thumb-
sucking
a lot of swelling
he swells — she swells
they all go down

Another First Kiss

~ after song lyrics by 'They Might be Giants'

When comes the time for me to slip this coil
of flesh — claimed by Death's everlasting kiss
I'll gladly step away from love's turmoil.
It matters not if I am grieved or missed,
for in this life you could not love me well —
to mourn me in my death would be too late.
Death beckons me: its song a lonely bell
and I — a dark swan searching for her mate.

Don't cry for me when all you caused was pain
each time you trifled with my eggshell heart.
I shall not wish to meet with you again
unless the sands of time skipped back to *start*.

Kiss me, my love — let's kiss away the past;
Now love me right — till Death cleaves us

Gardener’s Hands

I adore your broad hands — beaten
leather of your palms. They are gardener’s
hands, calloused from an honest weekend’s work, where
you have swapped your suits to plunge fingers into fecund
soil, planting riches for next moon’s harvest.

How I envy the earth
and her fulsome allure, swallowing
you without resistance. You thrust deep
into her marled moistness; she yields.
I long to take her place.

Beads of salt dot your temple, mawkish
in their primal tang. You grunt satisfied as an ox,
hooves clumped in loam, fertilising her.

I envy all this only because
you lovingly tend to a future
miles away
that does not include me.

Evaporated milk

Unconditional, so they say *(a mother's love, that is)*. But I've combed the T&Cs and — *spoiler alert!* — there is no such clause in any of the fine print.

I am a mother. That is, if I may be called a mother simply by virtue of having got myself up the duff, marinated a foetus in my oven, thereafter expelling the cooked lump of basalt-crusted sourdough most excruciatingly through an opening that seemed way too small for a head way, *waaaay* too big...that in fact, *was* WAY. TOO. BIG. Call it mother's instinct. Or science. Or whatever. No matter how much this watermelon tried to shove its galumphing self into the dainty glass slipper, it defied the laws of nature.

This insistent watermelon tore its own exit and slid out on a crimson riptide spewing forth the flotsam of redundant organs. A ridiculously large nine-pounder, so fully fleshed out, as though he had already lived one hundred and one newborn days.

The sucking, screaming, barely-sleeping creature clung to my breast like an ever-fattening leech, drugged to his eyeballs, drinking himself into milky stupor. Stirring scarcely hours later, he became a bleary-eyed addict with a five o'clock shadow, itching for another hit. *Who was I to argue with the punter?* I – me, my body – was open for service like a neon-lit gas station with a convenience-store-cum-diner annexed, brightly declaring: 24 hours a day, 7 days a week, all fucking year round.

An octo-limbed Ganesha, I became the establishment's barmaid, cleaner, jester, laundromat, *etcetera, etcetera, etcetera.* And when the creature's progenitor returned after hunting and gathering, I would slip into something a little more uncomfortable: the role of maid, chef, masseuse, glory hole, *etcetera, etcetera, etcetera.*

After seven hundred and thirty-one days, the offspring had learned to verbalise his thirst for boob juice. It was clear it was time for me to close the bar tab. He wailed and warbled like a demon possessed — in moments of maniacal withdrawal, clawing ribbons of pink-laddered flesh from my decolletage. All the while, a primitive part of my body still responded on instinct, despite my stony outward resolve. Each time he howled, milk would spit out of my swollen nipples as though it were on the multi-spray nozzle setting of a power hose from Bunnings.

More days passed. Four thousand three hundred and seventy-nine, to be exact. My spawn was now a hulking colossus. Still demanding, still regarding me a one-stop shop, still bleeding me dry. There are, in fact, limits to how much even a mother can take. Like the milk he had leached from my body as a bairn, greedily siphoning the calcium-rich marrow from my bowser, so too had he sucked away the last vestiges of the person I had been before him. I became brittle-boned, prone to splintering. And through the Tanami of my twilight years, I was left holding a beaten, leaking camel-leather hip flask, parched and wondering how all the love had evaporated.

Things I have done on a plane

This poem violates community standards.

It involved my hand, your lap, a blanket.

[Redacted] [Redacted] [Redacted]

Terracotta knuckles

I remember the game of knuckles we used to play as
kids in the dirt lane behind the old storage sheds,
corrugated rooves lined with squished

flesh of fermenting persimmons. I found it unsettling
the way we kept disembodied knuckles rattling around
inside old shoeboxes; though boxes

of severed limbs with knuckles intact would have been
even more disconcerting. They were painted in bold,
bright acrylics; eventually fading

with wear. The best ones were lacquered with nail
varnish — licks of shiny magic. I coveted these treasures
like a bower bird hoarding blue.

I still don't know where all the knuckles came from
— what hapless creatures had been mutilated to indulge
our childish whimsies. I retired early

from the game one blistering afternoon, crying foul over
a match. Stakes had been high — my prized polished
knuckle on the line for Tommy's flame-

tree beauty. I accused him of cheating; refused to hand over my knuckle. Detecting a glint of demon in his eye, I backed down; offered a rematch.

Without breaking his reaper's gaze, he prised the knuckle from my grip; knocked me to the ground. My punctured hymen splattered the drought, wetting

the earth's clay; terracotta pigment staining my dress, my clenched bone white knuckles. He instructed me to keep my *stupid trap shut* — said that if I squealed,

he would come *wee wee wee* to hunt me down; claim me all over again. Pocket the pretty little knuckle on my pinkie as his trophy.

Home is where the dark is

There are no sunflower smiles craning eager towards me
at arrival gates, beaming beacons so bright the pilot
can see the twinkling welcome from the turret
of the control tower, guiding us safely home.

There are no overpriced foil balloons on bendy stalks for me.
No sweet-faced boys clutching teddy bears clutching red heart-
shaped boxes filled with mushy-centred chocolates. No saccharine
declarations in wonky handwriting on cardboard banners
to make me wince with embarrassment
and secretly smile.

I glide home in darkness — *to* darkness,
pulling my baggage along; this battered
suitcase with its dickie wheel, squeaking self-
consciously along the uneven concrete
with each lop-sided revolution.

Vegas Cantina

We pull up bar stools in this digital cantina, speaking
the common language of HyperText tongues. This neon
Megacity never sleeps. Nor do I — my eyelids toothpicked
open to ogle the sensory overload. My guilty 2am fix
of 6 chicken nuggets **hell, make it 12 (YOLO!)**
medium fries **extra salty, extra hot** and a large ~~cock~~
coke. The city heaves and groans to the cheap
perfume of digital whores, dribbling
lips soliciting drunken orgies with sugar daddy doms. Mean-
while, the glitzy showroom proffers cat lolz, classical art
memes and kids saying the darndest things. *Shall I show you*
straight to the back door?

One may rent this love shack by the hour. What's the harm,
I think to myself. Just one more flutter, one more drink.
One more becomes *another more* until I'm pinned between
the legs of a faceless amour I know only by a screenname.
Like a sacrificial A.A. desert-dweller, I am thrust in the
Gladiator pit of a dizzying Vegas, drenched with more
delight than I can stand to drink. I hobble intoxicated,
as their skipping rope ellipses jump and quicken
to the beat of my gullible heart:

Cinderella, dressed in yellow
Went upstairs to kiss her fellow
Made a mistake
And kissed a snake
How many doctors
Did it take?
1, 2, 3, 4, 5…

Are you a snake, my love? I am delirious. You leave
little love bytes on my neck. Madness
begins to spread. You bloom viral under my skin.

Once upon a tale, in a love far away

~ A siren's long-distance lament

From petalled lips I long to sip sweet honeysuckle's wine
Strings of my corset loosening, libation spills my lust
On loam implanting roots with love — a wild Barossa vine
Oh, scatter seeds and yield to me, between my lips combust
Let slip your merlot down my throat and sate my greedy glut
For I am one athirst, adrift, delirious on a sea
Of salted tears I cannot drink, and therein lies the cut
The bottles blue as shells untouched: a sailor's remedy
When miles away from tangible caresses on one's skin
A buxom manatee wades by, with folds of slippery flesh
The sun beats down relentlessly; hallucination wins
You dive into the coolness, tumbling deftly with a splash
'Tis I, my love, I sing to you — come warm my watery bed
Forsake the other world you knew, come love with me instead.

This poem is in the form of a Sonnet in iambic heptameter, otherwise known as a 'Fourteener'.

Fifteen minutes in a studio backlot

(i)

The lady in the hair and makeup trailer had a name

I'd never heard before. It may have been Purdy. It may

not have been. But I recall having resisted the urge

to declare in a southern drawl *How purdy!* So I'm leaning

towards Purdy. Though maybe-Purdy's name has no real

bearing on this poem, so let's just cut to the next scene.

(ii)

Sitting in a gas-levered seat in front of a mirror

framed by Hollywood bulbs which (according to

the labels on the dual switch could be set to either

'white light' or 'daylight') my eyes roamed the shelves

stacked with palettes of eyeshadows, glosses, fake

lashes, rollers, and brushes as varied as cocks

in their array of sizes, applications, and peculiarities.

(iii)

Maybe-Purdy was gentle as she brushed out my knotted
tangle of frizz. The child in me silently willed her to brush
more briskly, to let me feel my mother's love yanking
at my hair with such perfunctory mettle that my scalp
would be raised by each white-knuckled root, each strand
a goose-pimpled pincushion of porcupine quills.

(iv)

Mother used to pull my hair into plaits so tight my oriental
eyes would turn into even slittier slants, so that I became
a caricature of myself — like those almond-eyed Disney
cats on *Lady and the Tramp,* jollying about singing
we are Siamese if you please. Some of us are stuck
being Siamese — even if we *don't* please.

(v)

Maybe-Purdy didn't turn me into an exotic feline.

With hands I'm guessing were well-practised

in *cat's cradle,* she used pinkies and forefingers

to deftly weave my hair into a loose French braid

then lathered a thick layer of foundation on my face

to make me look 'natural'.

(vi)

Later, I would visit my lover, who

yanked my hair and took a crop

to my arse. It was almost

more than my tender flesh

could stand. I fought

back tears and bore it

like a *good girl,* reminded

of what mother taught me

love   is   meant   to   hurt.

do-wah-diddy-diddy-dum-diddy-do

death steps up
to call his bluff

he played *chicken* on the regular
kawasaki revving
with the recklessness
of someone flicking a shiny silver
cigarette lighter
**click*   off   *click*   off*
right by a dripping petrol bowser
whilst the last drops
of ejaculate are shaken out
of the pump

beneath his wise-
cracking *pagliaccio* mask
i'd seen the dark
he tried to hide
it frightened me
my own felt seen

i know it's not enough
that i was never
enough. but i want to remind him
his existence matters
that i once cared
care
do
did

still do
urgh
can i start this over?

so here i am, rapid-firing bawdy
banter *(for old time's sake)*
because i want to cheer
him up, if only
for a moment — distract
him from his fresh death-
sentence
well gosh darn, lucky you sent me
these totally banal texts!
diagnosis?
virtually slipped
my mind

my ex lover is dying

although we didn't work out
it's complicated
or maybe not
just took me a while to get over
and i have a new lover now
i wish he wasn't
(dying)

Tourist Trap

(I) The price of first-world guilt

I walk down the narrow dirt laneway, flanked by raggedy green banana palms. To my left is a *bakso* cart, laden with soup and mie and tempeh, and rubbery balls of indistinguishable meat. The vendor has temporarily abandoned his stall and is now sitting in the nearby *Euro Bakery*, taking his time over an overpriced, oversized danish. Because he's now a customer, he may sit in the air-conditioning, escaping for a few precious minutes from the stinking humidity.

I am careful with my footing as I descend the sloped road where the gravel has come loose at the sides. I momentarily wonder whether I've pissed myself. It comes as a relief to know I have not — that the trickle of liquid running down my inner thighs are beads of sweat. A few steps later and I'm onto the main drag, where I am swallowed by a sea of tourists.

I pause at the corner, see a woman crouched on her hind quarters, two grubby children circling her in the way that children have of being interminably busy. She is clutching a crying bundle of rags. I wonder whether she has deliberately pinched the baby to assist in the loosening of foreign purse-strings. I push the unsavoury thought from my mind almost as fast as I push crumpled rupiah into the children's outstretched hands. *Sank yew,* they chime, well-versed in all the English they need to know.

(II) Ode to a bargain bin(tang) butt-plug

I reach the entrance of the open air markets — a maze of mass-produced trinkets: Bintang wife beaters, hanging plant cosies of strung-together shells, Bali Hai coasters featuring pictures of rice terraces and beaches, declaring: *wish you were here!* My glance hovers over a table crammed with collectibles. The hawk(er) senses my momentary hesitation — swoops in to entreat me: *Buy sexy souvenir? Buy for boyfriend?* I smirk at the thought of by-passing a more reverential memento in favour of this garishly painted, carved teak phallic-shaped bottle opener. Beside it is a smaller object of a similar ilk that could potentially pass as a wine-stopper. I purchase the latter.

Upon my return, I give you the gift. It is wrapped in rice-paddy-green tissue paper, with a recycled fibre batik notecard in which I have scrawled: *love is a many splintered thing.*

Cue Mancini's R+J theme song

Entwined in her embrace I gently stir
        As dappled sun falls through these drapes I've drawn
A single voice pulls me from my slumber —
        The quaver of a koel signals morn.
Oh, shush! Please go away I do implore;
        It surely cannot be the morning yet —
I long to stay with her I so adore
        Before she wakes and leaves and I forget
Her musk. The harshness of the light of day
        Casts shadows on the pleasures of the night:
I fear that from my life she'll slip away —
        Reality's a curse with no respite.
Each cuckoo call is thinning out my luck —
        Methinks she was just in it for a fuck.

Chaos rode into my life

on a shiny black Kawasaki

wearing tight trousers

and a crisp shirt. I should have looked

the other way. But his engine

was revving so loud it drowned

out all sense and I ached

to be purring alongside

his sculpted machinery.

Come for a ride he beckoned, tiger eyes

glinting with mischief.

I should have known better

than to go riding with Bacchus. My body — already

humming with heat — had its own fancies.

Straddling him between

my thighs, we soared

bareback down

the snaking

highway. Towards

disaster

or divinity?

I am

yet to find

either.

Simon Says

this game may hurt a little.

I yield to him anyway; he makes me feel special.

I am at that awkward age. These are still the times when we roam
the neighbourhood like strays, looking to be fed second helpings
of afternoon tea — especially if it's one of the days Mrs Thompson
has baked fresh scones

she'll serve up with jam she made from the mulberries we helped
collect in empty ice cream tubs from the tree in the council quadrangle.
Back doors remain unlocked. We let ourselves in through
flimsy flyscreen doors on sinking aluminium frames that need to be
jiggled with a little force.

It's a scorching summer's day. I'm too old to still be running around
under sprinklers in my cotton singlet and undies. I do anyway.
I like the feather-light droplets cooling my clammy skin. You are
a goshawk, perched on a deckchair under the lemon tree in your yard
next door, watching me with dilated

raptor eyes. When my rain dance eventually slows, you swoop —
towel at the ready, bundling me in a fluffy embrace that reminds me of
the seaside, with its nautical navy and white stripes. You have
led me to your couch where you rub the towel vigorously
up and down my slender arms, mussing

up my already tangled hair as I giggle over your exaggerated enthusiasm.
Are you cold? No, I reply. I follow your eyes tracking their way down to
my chest, where my budding breasts betray me —
little raisins straining erect against clinging fabric. *Better get you out of this*,

you say, pulling my singlet up over my head as I instinctively raise my arms.
I am now topless on your couch. You pat the towel lightly over my damp
chest. The towel has disappeared. In its place, your hands
now glide over my breasts.

You tell me you'd better inspect me more closely, as you slowly
bring your mouth to my honeyed skin, eyes fixed on mine. I am watching
you, watching me, as your lips circle and my body shivers
in response. Your hands trace down the gentle slope of my
underdeveloped waist; you pause

at the little satin bow in the centre of my white cotton underpants dotted
with blue butterflies. You finger the rim of the scalloped elastic.
Better take these off too, you say, slipping them down.

Simon says a lot of things
and I do all the things Simon says.

He touches me in special places.
It used to hurt. But now I think I like it.
His beard tickles my thighs.
He likes it when I laugh;
calls me beautiful.

Simon Says

don't tell anyone.

He rubs his special cream into my back
and pats my bottom

telling me to come
and play again soon.

Ma Mer, Maman

I find myself
here again
by the foaming mouth of the sea, listening
to her indecipherable whispers
shhhh.... *shhhh.....*
it's going to be okay

I come here
in times of distress
she comforts me
more than my cold birth
mother ever could

I nestle into the Oedipal womb of my longing
as she strokes my hair, silken as seaweed
singing lullabies:
hush, hush my darling—
come suckle in the wet of our mutual wanting
and I shall cradle you
till my bed runs dry

I dial his number on a buttercream rotary phone

Inhaling with each Everest of numbers scaled, exhaling with each spring-wound click-whirr of descent. I can do this, btw — *the rotary phone thing, that is* — because this is a dream sequence flashback of what *actually happened*. So here I am, in my mid-night desperation, wearing a sheer pink negligee with marabou feathers that adorn the bust and hem that skims mid-thigh *(because that is what ladies swan around in when we're at home alone, much like we do not snot-bubble-ugly-cry, so much as delicately dab away the mascara tracks that so prettily run down our tear-stained cheeks)*. Anyhoo … I am biting my lower lip, twirling the twisty plastic cord around my index finger, waiting for him—nay, *willing* him—to pick up the phone. It rings…and rings…four sequences of agonisingly drawn out *brrrrrriiiiinnng… brrrrrriiiiinnng…*{*crackle* *static*} — *perhaps it was five* — before I hastily slam down the receiver and wipe my sweaty palms on the chiffon, only now realising that I'd been holding my breath the entire ring cycle. I hiss a dejected exhalation, like a flaccid inflatable after the carnival is over.

Scanning my room for a suitable tool, my eyes fall upon a slim bamboo skewer. My previous implements have included paperclips *(only the standard metal kind, not those fancy plastic-coated ones that come in an array of fun colours)*, the pointy edge of a *Marshmallow*-scented tube of travel-sized hand cream, anything with even the slightest hint of a sharp edge can be used, really. I trace a light line onto my skin, to mark where I intend to etch. My hand wavers, hesitant to go deeper. Much as I crave release, I may have lost the nerve for this. I put the implement down — pick up this pen instead.

Autumn is so last season

A tree wielding heart-shaped leaves in strawberry and lemon and tangerine
hues stopped me in my tracks.   Autumn had not got the memo — Winter

had already presented for crossover: time to let go. But Autumn could not.
She knew why willows wept,   tender filaments,   suspended green in grief.

She fills   woven baskets   with remnants   of her splintered heart,   mini-
heartlets;   she is now   heartless,   hawking her wares   like a fishmonger

bearing a pebble-heavy yoke.

Hyde

and

Seek

You dive into the deep-
end of your mind where I cannot follow.
Given long enough, I may be able to fashion gills
out of the gutters you have gauged into my salmon-
pink flesh, still glistening wet and raw as sashimi, with the tail-
whip of your departure. I slink into the depths with my amphibious
air-tank; axolotl sporting a crown of stars. Move over Hedy; Esther;
there's a new silver-spleen goddess. With a mercurial flick of my mermaid fin,
I beckon ships with bellies full of thirsty sailors, splashing away melancholy until
I almost forget why I wept oceans at all.

Hotel Hoarder

I wish to remain anonymous in this confession of compulsive
hotel hoarding. It fills me with shame — though not enough
to stop me from stuffing my pockets with random bits of contraband.
Eagerly tearing open sachets as though they were condom wrappers
with their promise of a good time. Little packets of coffee, tea, sugar,
Equal — *I can't even explain the Equal* — never use the stuff; take it anyway.
Can't leave behind anything that's not bolted down. The bathroom
sweep nets tiny tubes of toiletries and more vanity kits than
I would ever need in a lifetime.

Why?? My mother's voice burrows into the vacant real estate
inside my head:

> *Because it's FREE. Your grandparents struggled through the war.*
> *They would have wanted you to take All The Things:*
> *shampoo, body lotion, shoe shine sponges; ephemera etcetera etcetera.*

Ah, but of course. Armed with this logic I stockpile little offerings to
appease my ancestors:

> *in spiritus sanctus to the Goddus Hoardus. Amen.*

But lo! One day I check in to my hotel to find the horror
of change. No more miniature bottles on the faux marble vanity.
Instead, great ghastly pump dispensers affixed to the wall: *for the sake
of the environment*, the label decrees, *to cut down on plastic
waste.* Like an addict deprived of a hit, I start sweating.
Momentarily consider whether I should subvert the system,
decant some of the soapy goop into my own empty shells
of tiny toiletries past.

But no! Little eyes are watching my hands as they waver.
Aren't you going to take that, Mum?
What am I doing to my children?

Grandfather's Clock

You stand — short and stout — much
like my grandfather, who gave you to me
when you died.
A time-keeper; no longer keeping
time. Your hands stopped moving
decades ago. They are painted
neon: glow-in-the-dark green
so you could always be seen. Petrified
in a mid-tock arabesque
of six thirteen. AM or PM, I wonder.
Surely the morn: of the little I know
of you, I know you woke up to the wassail of a koel each dawn.

Except for that morning you didn't.
Rusted slivers of the clock's innards
line its glass belly like ashes. My thumbprints disturb
dust that has settled over it like a fine muslin shroud.

Even without a pulse, I keep this memento.
Other things I inherited from you:
your punctuality
your gentleness
your snaggle-toothed smile.

I'm too dumb for poetry

I just don't get the poems that win the prizes. What is it I'm missing? To me, they are lacking in syntax and sense — jolty streams of cleverly curated consciousness in exaggeratedly elongated lines.

Too highfalutin for the likes of me, they're laden with in-jokes and I'm a teenager all over again, stuck minding the kids' table at a dinner party when the adults have started to bring out the port and whiskey.

> 'But look — I'm all grown up! I even have boobies to prove it!'
> 'Those balled up socks stuffed down the front of your top aren't fooling anyone, love.'

I scowl and burn and simmer, skulk back to my place in the communal dining hall of society. I bet I wouldn't even find their lah-di-dah oh-so-exclusive in-jokes funny even if I *did* get the punchline. These 'adults' are like critics at an art gallery, murmuring in awe, pretending to admire and decipher the hidden meanings of the artworks when really, the joke's on them—the pictures have been painted by baboons.

El Niño Verano

The air is thick with the humidity of another El Niño summer.
It is abnormally quiet for 4pm on a Sunday afternoon. Folk
don't have the energy to do much — *one can barely even exist* —

in this oppressive heat. It's underboob sweat kind of weather. I'm
tempted to pinch my mother's CPAP machine so that I might breathe
a little easier; stave off this creeping claustrophobia from mugginess

so dense you'd swear it was 3D. I lay on my bed like a starfish, gazing at
my shabby-chic sepia-toned clock bearing the image of an old-fashioned
bicycle with a wicker basket full of pink roses perched on the handlebars

and the word *Paris* in cursive font. It is lagging split-seconds behind
the beat because I haven't got around to replacing the batteries yet.
The slow revolutions of the blades of my dusty ceiling fan remind

me of submarine propellors. Or a merry-go-round. I conflate the
two and suddenly I'm imagining myself in the schoolyard as a child,
jumping between the blades of this subma-go-guillotine, Gladiator

style. But it is far too hot to be contemplating severed feet, so I pull
my mind away from such thoughts. The house yawns; stretches its
arthritic joints with cricks and creaks. Outside, an aeroplane hums

in the distance. Even the animals are silent. The washing on the line
would have dried hours ago, but it is too hot to go outside right now.
Sometimes I hear a flap of a billowing sheet or towel. When I collect

my laundry later on, the items are all crisp, as though tumble dried.
I like how they smell when they're extra crispy like this. I inhale
the sun. Soft branches of my mulberry tree lightly scrape like wire

drum brushes composing a laconic improv piece against peeling, sun-
faded weatherboards. Lulled into this makeshift jazz club, my thoughts
inevitably drift to you. When I think of you, my body responds. And

so, already slick with sweat on this sweltering Sunday afternoon, I add
to the chorus of *whirrr… ttock… flutter… scat…* with my body's own
music, as the southerly change sets in and the world hums back to life.

In a (blink)

When I close my eyes, I still see you
in every *Fruitopia*
kaleidoscope refraction.

When I close my eyes, I dream
of a Twister
of lips and tongues, fingers
raking like hair combs.
If I concentrate hard enough,
I can smell your *Paco Rabanne.*

When I close my eyes, I play
montages like a stop-motion
flipbook — from first kiss
to last
and everything
in between.

When I close my eyes, I trick myself
into imagining it didn't
end. And like a game of *Peekaboo,* when my eyes flutter
open the world
will be restored.

When I close my eyes, I remember how drunk
in love we were.
I can no longer stomach drinking —
or love.

When I close my eyes, I try to solve
the Rubik's cube
of where we went
wrong.

When I close my eyes, I fear
the Demogorgons
hunting me in their Up-
side Down.

When I close my eyes, blindfolded
by hooded vision
I perceive only
darkness.

When I close my eyes, our tapestries
are starting to fray
at the edges of my memory.
I fear you
will not exist
for much longer.

When I close my eyes, one day
I will find you
are no longer
there.

Pirates of the Andaman

My father was a man of few words. Except
when he released a story from his slow-
drip vault. His offerings would drop like shiny
coloured balls spun inside the giant metal cage
on the *Monday, Wednesday or Saturday Lotto* drawn
and televised live at 8.45pm on Channel 7TWO.
We'd listen with *tarsier* eyes as a tale from his past
would roll smoothly along the curved pipework and plop
into our laps like missing parts of a 10,000 piece jigsaw
puzzle. We were only 8,271 pieces short.

They weren't the kind of bedtime stories suitable
for the tender ears of children. Still — there are things
that haunt us no matter what age. We carry these ghosts
with us, carefully cradling them in still-wet gauze
like miscarried babies swaddled. *Shhhhh…hush now…..*

Across oceans of time, the faceless foetuses squirm
under restless currents, reeking like shrimp paste sludge
leaking out the bottom of a busted garbage bag. These
were back-alley stories, of things we dared not utter
outside the pinky promise safety of our immediate
flesh and blood.

I whisper them now, in Pollock-veiled abstractions
(some of the characters are still alive). Like the cousin
who liked that *other cousin* a little too much. The latter
disappeared for several months — to take in fresh
country air, it was explained. How very Austen-esque.

The provincial sawmill empire—*and with it, my grandparents' entire fortune*—going up in flames when my father was knee-
high to a grasshopper. It can't have been easy to have gone
from private carriage to cattle-class. I'll spare them the indignity
of airing the next socks and jocks in this story — whose souls
needed to be bartered at the black market, and at what cost.

My father as a child in hospital, squeezing tight his almond
eyes and his mother's spider-veined hand at the sound of the nurse's
rubber-soled sneakers squeaking up the bleached linoleum
hallway to administer his daily injection. The vaccine
for *polio* was introduced shortly after. But it was too late
for him. He has been limping through life ever since.

Father told us of shiploads of Viet fleeing like rats from their war-
torn country. Pragmatic decisions had to be made *(strictly off-record).* Sink the ships. Two of them, at first. As a warning.
Nobody was to be spared — not the men, not the women,
not the children. Warnings needed to be unequivocal.

Then —

and this was meant to be the genius of the plan — these very officials,
with their stained military gloves, would start spreading their own
rumours. *Turn back! Turn back now! There are pirates circling these seas.
Two ships have already been attacked! No survivors! Seek refuge elsewhere.*

It was then that my father — a man of few words, packed his life
into one scuffed suitcase. No longer able to bear silent
witness, he left the sanctuary of his mother-
country, in search of a compass for a nation's misplaced morals.

Subliminal

I wasn't expecting to find you here — in this liminal
stillness. No armour. We have softened. Firetail finches scatter
the siphoned remnants of our song like sun shafts blind to shadow.

This poem employs a Korean form: the Sijo.

Dear Patient #23 from Ward 17

You paced these grounds a century before me.
During supervised breaks, of course. They let you out for a daily
dose of air and exercise. You'd take off your shoes to feel the grass under
your feet — absorbing the *real* of damp earth. Inside,
the floors were scrubbed so sterile
your nostrils burned from the bleach. They sanitised *everything* —
floors, furniture, souls.
I imagine the sunshine did your spirit good as it is currently doing mine.
I spend too much time
indoors, chained to my desk and chores. Churlish of me to complain,
I know
when you spent your days chained to the bed, enduring horrors
both medically sanctioned *and* off the books.

Wandering towards the waterfront below, I pause midway
on an embankment. I don't suppose they would have let you go all the way
down. I perch myself at the foot of what was once a stone fountain —
now parched;
fancy myself having a picnic with you at this over-hanging rock,
both of us wearing
whimsical white dresses. The ground is carpeted with brittle brown
leaves that must have been shed by the tree overhead,
its spindly branches clawing
at the vast expanse.

Blow back

I drove past your house today, for the first time in months — still
there on its unassuming corner, looking as it had always looked, though
different somehow; changed. White picket paling gate ajar, I resisted
the urge to collect junk mail rolled up in your lopsided letterbox, to tread
the smooth-pebbled path and peer in through the flyscreen
like the first time we met, when rapture greeted us
wide-eyed at the door.

Was *she* home, I wondered. Did she even live there anymore? I'd known
you'd moved months ago. Hoped it was to feather our love nest
in your inner-city penthouse. It was still
so naked when you first took me there.
Not even a bed. You took me
over the balcony, pressed against windows and walls,
on the floor — getting carpet
burn. A 'For Lease' sign told me more than you ever did.
I wasn't sure whether you'd got back with her. I guess not.

The last time I was here, down at this beach on a summer's day not
unlike this, we were fucking. The waves have crept higher now: a bashful
ex-lover pulling the sheath of her tide over the exposed bed of jelly-
fish limbs; slippery rockpools you once swam in. Even sightless, sub-
merged, you remember how good I once felt tangled between your legs.

The last time I saw you, you were riding away on your Kawasaki
L plates flapping in the ocean breeze, freedom
ballooning like your wind-swept shirt.
You never looked back.

This town has nothing left for either
of us. It is a seaside ghost town; a carnival
abandoned by seasonal merry-makers
making merry elsewhere.

A trail of lovelorn shells whisper of what they once witnessed in halcyon times:

Of the wife you loved and lost
Of the dreams you built and sold
Of a summer fling with a foolish girl
who still thinks of you, long after
her footprints have been washed away.

We are Saguaro
Last of the Yaquis

Perhaps love can nest within me yet
A rosy-cheeked *Gila Woodpecker* finds his way under my skin
I am harbouring a lover
I have a secret
Doesn't mean I enjoy the drought
Just because I *can* survive in the Sonoran Desert
Everyone keeps their distance
It appears I wish to be left alone
Prickly right through to my pulp
Who could love me like this?
I drink in my hairy arms
Madre is right
[She wants to keep me to herself]
We are tough — don't need nobody
We are Saguaro, mija
Madre told me so
I was born to be alone

This is a Reverse poem; the nuance shifts depending on whether it is read from top to bottom or bottom to top.

Cherry Soda Pop

> ***'You'll ache. And you're going to love it. It will crush you.***
>
> ***And you're still going to love all of it.***
>
> ***Doesn't it sound lovely beyond belief?'***
>
> ***~ Ernest Hemingway 'The Garden of Eden'***

It is crushing. Like that time when I was seven and my father backed our bottle-
green Volvo sedan into the driveway over a speedbump that should not have been
there. I know I shouldn't have looked, but I couldn't help it. Mack's squished

little body like someone had tripped and spilled cherry soda pop
in snow. Dad had to scrape minced bits of Mack out of the grooves
of our tyres with an old toothbrush. It took weeks for the unnaturally

bright splatter to fade from the concrete completely. Even then, a bleached
halo reminded us of the pain we had tried to scrub away. Perhaps that is why
they call it a *crush*. Perhaps I should look away this time.

Ceviche

Your little yuzu sapling should have tipped me off to your love
of zest. You tended to it with the care and patience of a zen
master cultivating inner peace. I have begun craving the tart tang

of tangerine tickling my tastebuds, imagining you on my tongue as
I dip into the pink flesh of a grapefruit wedge — sweet, bitter and
sourish — bright as a sharp slap prickling pungent as smelling salts.

My lips pucker as I suck the rind bare as my cunt — a slow kiss laced
with a lick of vinegar. Love flays me — I tingle. My senses awaken to
you; the blood orange dribbling acidic into each tiger stripe of my

wounds. I become an ouroboros, consuming my own marrow,
marinating in your secretions. I am raw — my translucent flesh
transformed by the lime of your love.

I wanted to write you a love letter

~ Ode to an Ode *(an Abecedarian [A-Z] poem)*

All the letters in the world—infinite Scrabble
blocks begging to be arranged into poetry. Still, I fall mute —
cannot claw my way out of igneous overwhelm to
distil the lustrous
essence of a glinting tiger's eye: the enigma of you.
Forgive me, my love — I wished to
give you more than this.
Here — in the meantime, take this
instead:
joy to bring the sweetness of summer's first cherries to your days;
kisses to add lashings of hot *Sriracha* to your nights.
Love, love and even
more love. Sprinkle on that parmesan of love. Too much will
never be enough.
Oh, my darling — let me love you to life:
profusely and passionately, without
question or qualm.
Reach into my constellations — hidden galaxies I keep
secret, safe, shatterproof inside my
triple-bolted heart. I will show you a
universe
vibrant as a new dawn, fresh
with the promise of possibility.

xoxo
Yours always, from A to
Z

Lunar Lovesong

She sits on the ledge of her bone-
white windowsill, watching the elms scratch
out love notes like *Sissipahaw* smoke-
signals scribbled into inked sky parchment.

The moon is full as her milky breasts
nudging plump against the unresisting
silk of her lilac chemise. Head tilted
in reverie, her fingers comb through
sooty thickets of waves, weaving
plaits like a milliner's daughter.

Under the same sky, miles away, he dreams
odes to her on the shimmering skipjack-
scale surface of a lunar-dipped sea.
Beneath the gleaming undulations, silver-
missile minnows and weavers scribe
his lovesongs in the sand. The moon keeps
weaving at her sky-loom, pulling the ebb
and flow of tidal threads into eternal
bindings of lovers' knots.

Barefoot Poetess

There is not much I have to offer you, my love —
I am threadbare, travelling light through this
darkness with my knapsack of precious little,
wandering in search of a heart to call home.

I could give you my monastery,
though it is on lease. When winter nips
at the buds of my breasts, nature will come
to cash in on the rent. Enjoy the cornucopia
of now, but love me for more than my hollow husk.

Love the thorny parts of me; they will endure beyond the first
flush of foxgloves. Love my volcanic intensity, splitting open
the earth's core like a perfectly poached thunderegg,
drenching you with silken yolk. When you hear
the susurrus of verdant fronds, my darling, my cheer-
leader pom poms will quiver your name.

I will give you this poem — and many more.
I will plant my roots in you and call you home.

Paris Rosemont

Paris Rosemont is much more than the sum of the labels society tries to box her into. She will bust her way out of the *coffin [in which she strains] against tightly coiled serpentine springs*, exploding in *dazzling colour pops* of verse all over your white-washed linens. If you'd like to know more about this 'wildest of wildcards', simply read her poetry. It's all there.

www.parisrosemont.com

Paris' 2023 debut collection *Banana Girl* received the 'Distinguished Favorite' Award in NYC Independent Press Awards 2025 (USA), was shortlisted for the *Association for the Study of Australian Literature's* 2024 Mary Gilmore Award, 2024 Eyelands International Book Awards (Greece) and The Society of Women Writers NSW, and longlisted for the 2024 International Poetry Book Awards (UK).

My heartfelt thanks

I was not prepared for the reality slap of life as a poetess. Surely, devoting myself to pursuing something I loved would make life a joy, right? *Right??!!* Of course, there have been many moments that have been indescribably joyous, creatively inspiring, and emotionally enriching. But it has also been intensely gruelling – mentally, emotionally, and financially. Many times, the very thing I loved threatened to be the very thing that broke me. But I kept going. And here I am—just over a year after my debut collection *Banana Girl* was released into the world, with my second collection freshly minted. I feel as though I have grown a lot in that time—both personally and poetically.

My heartfelt thanks to the *Association for the Study of Australian Literature* for shortlisting *Banana Girl* for the *2024 Mary Gilmore Prize.* It was an incredible honour. You were the first industry body to recognise my debut collection as a work of significance that held merit and meaning within the Australian literary landscape. Your judges' report brought me to tears.

Thank you to the *International Poetry Book Awards (UK), Eyelands International Book Awards (Greece)* and *The Society of Women Writers NSW Inc.* for long and shortlisting *Banana Girl* for your *Poetry Book Awards 2024.* Thank you also to the *NYC Independent Press Award 2025 (USA*) for awarding *Banana Girl 'Distinguished Favorite'.*

I would like to thank the following journals, zines and anthologies, in which some of my poems in this collection were first published: Apples: an unapologetic anthology from the core, Authora Australis, Blue Bottle Journal, FemAsia Magazine, FERAL: a journal of poetry & art, Gems zine (VIC), Jacaranda Journal (UQP), Live Encounters Poetry & Writing, Openbook (State Library of New South Wales), Paper Cranes Literary Magazine, Poetry d'Amour 2024 (WA Poets),

Red Room Poetry, The Salons, Seasons: Romanian and Australian Anthology of Contemporary Poetry & Prose, Short Stories Unlimited, Sky Island Journal (USA), Splinter Journal (SA), Written Off, 34-37 degrees south (South Coast Writers Centre).

Thank you to my incredible mentor – Pulitzer Prize nominee Dorianne Laux, who enlivened my senses to the beauty and richness within my personal universe. With her discerning eye, Dorianne helped me to amputate 50+ poems from my first iteration of *Barefoot Poetess* so that what remained would be given enough breathing space to truly shine.

I would like to thank the following publications who have published my poems this past year or so which do not appear in this collection. Perhaps some of these poems may find their way into my next book. For now, they have wonderful homes in the following places: Allium: A Journal of Poetry & Prose (USA), As Alive Journal (Canada), Australian Poetry Journal, Bronze Bird Books (USA), Chameleon (Auburn Poets & Writers), Cigarette Fire Literary Magazine, Clever Fox Literary (USA), Dark Poets Prize II, Flying Islands '100 Poets', Gypsophila, International Proverse Poetry Prize Anthology 2024 (Hong Kong), Persephone Literary Magazine (USA), Prosetrics (Amsterdam),The Quarter(ly) (USA), Rabbit (RMIT), Verge Literary Journal 2024 (Monash University).

Thank you to the incredible judges who spend so much time, effort, and care reading and considering extraordinary amounts of poetry. I am grateful that you saw fit to award my poems the following:

Blow back, do-wah-diddy-diddy-dum-diddy-do, doppelgänger dildo, I dial his number on a buttercream rotary phone and *Simon Says:* shortlisted for the *Born Writers Award #4*

Dear Patient #23 from Ward 17 & *Proshchaniye, Ms Karenina:* shortlisted for the *Born Writers Award #3*

I wanted to write you a love letter: runner-up in the *Vocal Abecedarian Challenge* (USA)
In a (blink): commended in the *Short Stories Unlimited Open Themed Poetry Competition 2024*
Kill the Wabbits: longlisted for the *New Writers Poetry Competition 2024 (UK)*
Ma Mer, Maman: first prize in the *Hammond House Publishing Origins Poetry Competition 2023 (UK)*
Pirates of the Andaman: second prize in the *Whitsundays Literary Heart Awards 2024 Poetry Prize*

Being able to share my poetry with audiences through the intimacy, cadence, and ephemeral nature of live performance has been an utter joy! Thank you to the following festivals for inviting me to perform: EnQueer (Sydney Queer Writers' Festival, for which I was also a guest curator), Mudgee Readers' Festival, Red Dirt Poetry Festival (Alice Springs), Short+Sweet Festival (Sydney), Words on the Waves Writers Festival (Central Coast), and an anticipatory thank you to the Newcastle Writers' Festival for inviting me to feature in your 2025 program.

Thank you also for inviting me to feature: Arts & Tarts Radio Show, Cabaret Eclectique, The Creative Ticket Podcast, Culture Club Poets, Kink in the Tale, Literature Live, Pie in the Sky Poets, Poetica Petit, South Coast Writers Centre, Sydney Poetry Lounge, WestWords Academy Live! Special thanks to the Sydney Fringe Festival for inviting me to be a judge for the 2024 season.

I am incredibly grateful to have been awarded creatively enriching residencies with Atelier Artist in Residence (Ireland), Barrett House

Creative in Residence (Randwick City Council), Kathmandu International Artist in Residence (Nepal), KSP Fellowship (WA) on full scholarship, Lighthouse Arts Writers' Residency (Newcastle), and the inaugural Nan Tien Temple / South Coast Writers Centre Writers' Residency.

I'd like to acknowledge the special projects and exhibitions some of my poetry has been featured in. Thank you to Lighthouse Arts for showcasing my poetry as part of the *Elemental* exhibition and to the Hunter Writers' Centre for your constant support and encouragement, Randwick City Council for hosting my Barrett House end of residency solo poetry exhibition and showcase, and for awarding me a Community Creative grant that made it possible for me to bring my Poet in the House audio recordings and Masterclasses + Workshops to life, and to The Salons and Poetry Sydney for inviting me to be part of the incredible Vessels of Love: love in transmission 2024 multimedia poetry project. The care and sensitivity with which you engaged with me, and my work, was so very much appreciated.

My heartfelt thanks to those who have nurtured me and my poetic journey through your friendship, guidance, support, and presence: ali whitelock, Augusta Supple, Brad McNeil, Dorianne Laux, Helen Hopcroft, Jennifer Compton, Jo Karaolis, Judith Beveridge, Kit Kelen, Laurie May, Mark Tredinnick, Margo Hofmann, Peter Hollo, Ruth Warren, Sarah Minchin, Stella Clarke, and Tim Loveday. You all took a chance on me, in some shape or form. And you turned up for me when I needed you, no matter what the weather. I am so grateful to you all.

Thank you to my fellow WestWords Academy Alumni with whom I have shared many heart to hearts — especially Adam, Jelena, Joanne,

Hemat, Luke and Shannon. Thank you also to all the gorgeous souls who support me by coming to my shows, buying my books, attending my classes, and reaching out to me with kindness.

Special thanks to Matt Houston from Ironbark Photography for capturing an amazing array of photographs of the various onstage faces I pull and stances I strike, right from my very first gig as a performance poet and beyond. Your continued encouragement and support has meant a lot to me.

To my children, Oliver and Darcy: please forgive your mama for having flown away with the mockingbirds for a while. You noticed something was amiss, when others did not. I am glad we survived the most volatile of times. You are two of the reasons I remain here today.

I may not have ventured quite so far, quite so quickly, in my poetic journey had it not been for the incredible support of my publisher, WestWords, and its vigorous team: Michael Campbell, Ally Burnham and Beau Quilty. WestWords has supported my emergence as a poet in so many ways, right from the very beginning. I recall sitting in Michael's office on the verge of a nervous breakdown one day, because the precarious nature of life as a creative was wearing me down. He said to me gently: *it is a difficult path you've chosen. But rather than giving up on it completely, you need to learn to rest when you need to.* And so, I keep walking this path, barefoot but happier than I've ever been.

Finally, thank you to my dearest, darling everything. I wanted to write you a love poem. This book, and the *barefoot poetess* of its title, is yours.